LET'S PLAY AN INSTRUMENT

LET'S PLAY AN INSTRUMENT

A Music Book for Kids

Rachelle Burk

Illustrated by Junissa Bianda

ROCKRIDGE PRESS

For general information on our other products and services, please contact our Customer Care Department within the United States at (866) 744-2665, or outside the United States at (510) 253-0500.

Paperback ISBN: 978-1-63878-736-5
eBook ISBN: 978-1-63878-925-3

Manufactured in the United States of America

Interior and Cover Designer: Heather Krakora
Art Producer: Janice Ackerman
Editor: Laura Bryn Sisson
Production Editor: Emily Sheehan
Production Manager: Jose Olivera

Illustration © 2022 Junissa Bianda

Author photo courtesy of Alana Barouch

10 9 8 7 6 5 4 3 2

To Leslie and Chad:
The beat goes on.
~RB

It's time to get ready for the concert!
Let's try out a few instruments.
There are many to choose from.

Big or small. Narrow or tall.
Some you blow into.
Some you bang or clang.
Others you pluck or strum.

They jingle.
They boom.

They trill and du-doom.

They whistle.
They sing.

They tootle and pling!

Which instrument
is right for you?

These instruments all have strings.
They make music when their strings move
back and forth very fast, or **vibrate**.

Thicker strings make
lower sounds.

Thinner strings make
higher sounds.

Some string instruments are played by plucking or strumming.

Others are played with a *bow*—a wooden stick with horsehair stretched from end to end.

Let your fingers or bow dance across the strings!

A guitar has six strings.
The long, thin part is
called the neck.

You can play different
groups of notes, called **chords**,
by holding down the strings
on the neck with your fingers.

You pluck or strum the
strings over the hole with
your other hand
or with a **pick.**

You can sing along as you play!

A violin has four strings. To hold the instrument, tuck the bottom between your chin and shoulder.

The violin is played with a bow. Push and pull the bow across the strings.

The harder you press the bow,
the louder the sound. In an orchestra,
the violin is the center of attention!

Zinga-zinga-zing!
Zin-zin-zin!

The music whispers
and shouts, leaps
and sways.

The ukulele looks like a baby guitar. But don't be fooled! It has its own sound and personality.

Dingle - dingle

Twingle-ingle-ing!

Ukuleles come in four sizes, each with only four strings. You play chords with one hand and strum or pluck with the other.

The ukulele plays high, dainty notes.

The bass is the biggest string
instrument. It is taller
than most grown-ups!
You must stand behind it
or sit on a high stool
to play it.

Like the violin,
it has four strings
and is played
with a bow.
The bass makes
very low notes.

Zoom-baa,
Zoom-baa,
Zoom-zoom
baaah!

Its deep voice rumbles
like a train rolling down the tracks.

The string players are warming up.
Who will help keep the rhythm?
That's what the percussion section does.

These instruments make sounds when
you strike, shake, or rub them.
Some have inside parts that move
against different parts to make a sound.
Others vibrate when you strike them
with your hands or other objects.

Pit-a-pat, rat-a-tat-tat!
Chicka-chicka, ding-a-ling!

CRASH!

Cymbals and drums. Triangles and bells.
Rattles, maracas, and xylophones!
Even whistles and wind chimes are
percussion instruments.

A tambourine is a type of small drum on a round frame. It has jingly metal discs around the sides called *zils*.

You can hit it,
shake it, and jiggle it!
You can even smack it on your
hip while you dance and sing.

Jingle-jangle,
Shicka-shicka-shicka!

The tambourine is
one of the easiest
instruments to play
and can be
taken anywhere.

Bass, snare, bongos, and congas!
There are many kinds of drums to choose from.

When you hit the drum head with your hand or
a stick, it vibrates and makes a sound.
Sometimes you feel it as much as you hear it!

Drums roll, rumble, and boom like thunder.

A maraca is a big rattle filled
with beans, beads,
or pebbles. It is also called
a rumba shaker.

Maracas are usually
made of wood or
a hollowed gourd.
They are often used in
pairs—one in each hand.

Hold one by the narrow handle
and shake, shake, shake!

Shaka-
shaka,

Cha-cha-
cha!

Mark the beat
as the music plays!

The piano is a percussion instrument
because little hammers inside it
hit strings when you play.
But it belongs to other families, too.

It is also a string instrument
because the strings vibrate
to make the sound. It is a keyboard
instrument because of its 88 keys.

Plink-a-link-a-link!
Lalala!

Let your fingers tickle the keys!

So you're not a strummer? Not a drummer?
Try a woodwind instrument!

All woodwinds are hollow tubes with holes.
Your breath is the wind that makes the music.

When you blow into the mouthpiece, a sliver of wood called a **reed** vibrates to make the sound. Different notes flow out when you open and close the holes with your fingers.

The flute has a different note
for every one of its 16 holes.

Hold it out to one side and blow into
the mouthpiece. It's like making a sound
by blowing into a bottle. The flute has
the highest voice of all the woodwinds.

The notes flutter and fly through the air like little birds.

The clarinet is a woodwind instrument with eleven holes. You can play it while sitting or standing, or while marching or dancing!

Gently blow into the mouthpiece. The wide end where the sound comes out is called the *bell*.

Hoodle-doodle hoodle-det hoodle-doodle-doodle-doo!

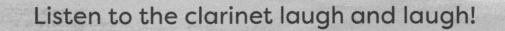
Listen to the clarinet laugh and laugh!

The saxophone is so cool
that it even has a nickname: sax.
Its shape is curvy and fun,
like its jazzy music.

The saxophone
has 23 to 25 holes,
depending on the kind of sax.
You open and close the holes
by pressing the keys
with your fingers.

Now, sway with the music.

The bell sends the warm, smooth notes flowing up, up, and away.

Hong-hong
Hoo-wee-hoo

wee-oom!

Most woodwinds have a single reed.
But the oboe has a double reed that you
blow across to make the sound.

The instrument is made of wood and has
23 holes. You play different notes by
pressing the keys to open and close the holes.
The oboe's song is bright and clear.

Wee-oh, eeee-oh!
Wee-oh, eeee-oh!

It sings a sad,
sweet tune.

It's almost concert time!
Call in the audience
with the clear, booming voices
of the brass section.
Brass instruments are
shiny horns made of metal.

Their bodies are hollow tubes
curled up like sleeping snakes.
At the end is a wide bell where
the sound comes out.

Press your lips against the mouthpiece.

Now

BLOW

like you're
filling a balloon or
blowing a raspberry!

The trumpet's voice is high and loud.
It hollers, *HERE I AM!*

To play, press your lips together
and blow hard into the mouthpiece.
The trumpet has three **valves** that
you press to make different notes.

Although it is the smallest of all the brass instruments, it sounds like a huge elephant!

Once you try the smallest brass instrument, why not try the biggest? The tuba is a gentle giant. Its body curls around and around.

It has three valves that you work with your fingers as you blow. The tuba bellows out its low, mellow music.

It sounds just like a loud, deep yawn after a long nap!

Oom-pah! Oom-pah!

Oom-pah-pah!

The trombone doesn't have
keys or valves like other brass instruments.
Instead, it has a long, U-shaped *slide*
to play the notes.

Pull it in for high notes. Push it out
for low notes. In and out, in and out.
STRETCH your arm as
far as you can!

Eeeh-oooh! Oooh-eeh!
Waah-waah-waah!

The sound is deep,
strong, and powerful.

The audience has gathered. It's time to play.
Which instrument will you choose?

A drum?
A trombone? The smooth saxophone?

♪ Will you strum,
shake, or blow? ♫

Use a stick or a bow?

Will you dance, sit, or stand?
Maybe march in a band?

Play salsa or Bach,
snazzy jazz or hard rock?

Join in with your friends.
The instruments sound
even better when we all
play together!

ABOUT THE AUTHOR

Rachelle Burk writes fiction and nonfiction for children ages 3 to 13, including Rockridge Press titles *The Story of Simone Biles* and *Stomp, Wiggle, Clap, and Tap: My First Book of Dance*. A retired social worker, Rachelle also entertains children as Tickles the Clown and Mother Goof Storyteller. As an author, she visits schools across America. You can find out more about her books and school visits at RachelleBurk.com.

ABOUT THE ILLUSTRATOR

Junissa Bianda has been creating whimsical illustrations for children's books since she graduated with her master of fine arts degree from the Academy of Art University in San Francisco. In addition to illustrating more than 25 books from well-known publishers over the last 5 years, she debuted her first written and illustrated book series titled *Kareem and Khaleel* in 2021 and the third book from that series will be published in late 2022. To find out more of her works, you can go to JunisStudio.com.

Printed in the USA
CPSIA information can be obtained
at www.ICGtesting.com
CBHW041315280124
3678CB00009B/12